When baby is unwell it can be very distressing, not only for baby but also for his carers. Many baby illnesses and ailments pass quickly, and need little or very simple treatment, but others require medical attention, sometimes urgently. It is natural to worry when all is not right. **Baby Health** is intended to provide you with background advice and information. It is **not** intended to replace the advice of your doctor. Now you are a parent it is very important to have a doctor or medical practice that you like and trust and can call on when your baby is sick or when you are concerned.

This book is about babies in their first 12 months, and thus covers only some illnesses, infections and conditions likely to affect this age group. Illnesses more likely to affect older children are not included.

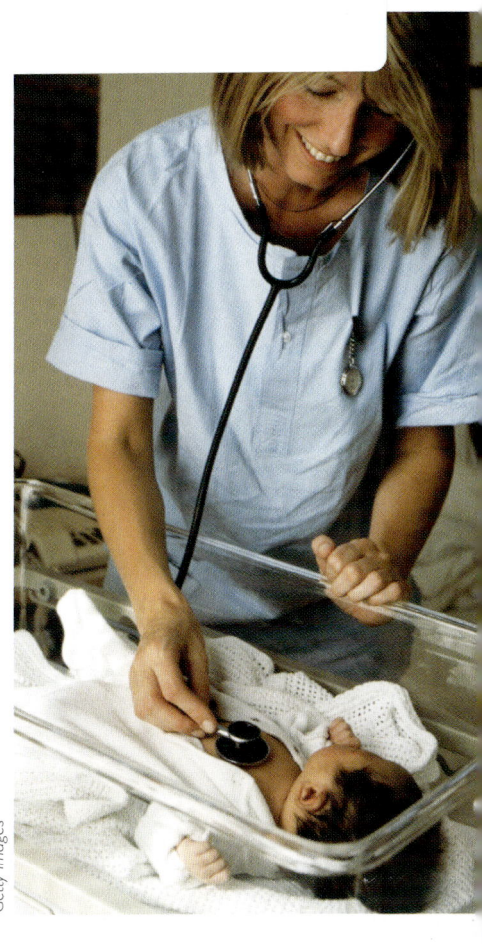

Getty Images

Disclaimer: *While every care has been taken in the preparation of this book, readers are advised to seek professional advice if in doubt about any aspect of their baby's health. Neither the author nor the publisher may be held liable for any action or claim resulting from the use of this book or any information contained herein.*

contents

keeping baby healthy	4	Dislocation	28
		Diphtheria	28
giving your baby medicine	6	Drowning	28
		Ear problems	31
immunisation	8	Eczema	31
		Encephalitis	32
common baby ailments	10	Eye problems	32
		Fever	33
Abdominal pain	10	Finger injuries	34
Allergies	10	Foot problems	34
Anaemia	10	Fractures	34
Antibiotics	12	Gastric reflux	36
Aspirin	12	Gastroenteritis	36
Asthma	13	Genital problems	37
Bites and stings	14	Giardiasis	37
Animal bites	14	Head injuries	38
Insect bites	14	Heart murmurs	38
At the beach	17	Heat problems	39
Taking a temperature	17	Hepatitis	40
Breathing problems	18	Hernia	40
Bronchiolitis and bronchitis	18	HIV infection and AIDS	41
Burns and scalds	20	Hives	41
Chickenpox	21	Impetigo	41
Choking	21	Influenza	42
Coeliac disease	22	Intestinal obstruction	42
Colds	23	Leg problems	44
Colic	23	Lumps and swellings	44
Conjunctivitis	23	Measles	44
Constipation	24	Meningitis	44
Convulsions	24	Mouth problems	46
Cradle cap	24	Mumps	47
Dehydration	26	Nose problems	47
Diarrhoea	26	Pneumonia	47

Poisoning	48	Teething	52
Poliomyelitis	48	Tetanus	54
Pollution effects	49	Thrush	54
Rashes	50	Urinary tract infections	55
Roseola infantum	50	Vaginal infections	56
Rubella	50	Viruses	56
Scabies	51	Vomiting	56
Scarlet fever	51	Whooping cough	57
Shock	51	Worms	58
Sneezing	52		
Splinters	52	help	60
Suffocation	52	index	62
Sunburn	52		

Getty Images

keeping baby healthy

Your love is a very important part of your baby's growth and development – babies thrive on cuddles, hugs and attention. They also need you to provide them with the right food – breast milk or infant formula, followed by a gradual introduction to family foods – and a warm, clean environment.

Your new baby will be susceptible to infections, particularly colds – and more so if she is in regular contact with a number of people, especially other children.

 Children under five get an average of eight colds a year.

THINGS YOU CAN DO TO HELP MINIMISE THE NUMBER OF INFECTIONS YOUR BABY GETS:

★ Be scrupulous about hygiene. Simply washing your hands in warm soapy water for at least 30 seconds after you have changed baby's nappy or used the toilet yourself, or petted an animal, and whenever you blow your nose or sneeze, will reduce the risks.

★ Be equally scrupulous about handwashing before you prepare any of baby's food (or your own). Be aware of food safety – never use the same utensils or implements for raw and cooked food; always store cold food below 4°C; keep hot food hot.

★ Do your best to ensure that baby's environment is healthy. Keep her away from cigarette smoke to reduce her risk of developing asthma, bronchitis and other respiratory problems.

★ Feed baby according to her needs, keep her warm and comfortable and try to ensure she gets the sleep she needs.

Viktorija Macens

BABY HEALTH

giving your baby medicine

Most babies will need to be given medicine of some kind in their first year. Your doctor will show you how to administer it, but don't be afraid to ask questions, or to call if you are unsure what to do once you are on your own.

HERE ARE A FEW IMPORTANT TIPS:

★ Never give a baby under 12 months of age over-the-counter medicine from the pharmacy or supermarket unless you have been specifically told to do so by your family doctor. Babies can very quickly go into overload, on even simple over-the-counter preparations, and this can cause more problems.

★ If your doctor has prescribed or recommended a medicine for your baby, follow the instructions very carefully. The medicine may need to be shaken before you give it to baby. Always use a proper medicine measure (a dropper or a medicine glass) so that you give the correct dose. Kitchen spoons vary so much that they are not suitable.

★ Follow the directions on the container about where to store the medicine — it may need to be kept in the fridge.

★ If baby seems to be reacting to the medicine — that is, if she is showing side-effects — talk to your doctor as soon as possible. If you cannot make contact within four hours, stop

giving baby the medicine until you can get in touch.

★ If an antibiotic has been prescribed, be sure to complete the course. However, don't give baby other medicines for any longer than the period prescribed by the doctor.

★ Never give someone else's medicine to your baby (or baby's medicine to anyone else, for that matter).

★ Never give your baby any products which contain aspirin.

★ Never keep a medicine which is past its use-by date – return it to your pharmacist, who has facilities for the disposal of unused medicine.

GIVING YOUR BABY MEDICINE

immunisation

Immunisation has saved many, many lives. In Britain, for example, before immunisation against diphtheria was introduced, the disease was contracted by one child every 15 minutes, and one child died of it every five hours.

Since 1970, when the diphtheria vaccine became available, there have been only nine deaths. One child in every 10 who contracts whooping cough also contracts pneumonia; about four in every 1000 sufferers will also suffer brain damage from convulsions.

Whooping cough can also kill. The scare campaign against the whooping cough vaccine has no basis in fact.

Immunisation schedules differ slightly from country to country. The current schedule for Australian children is set out on the opposite page. Many local councils run immunisation programs which undertake to advise you when the next immunisation is due.

The immunisations are all by injection except for the Sabin vaccine against poliomyelitis, which is given by mouth. Severe reactions are very rare.

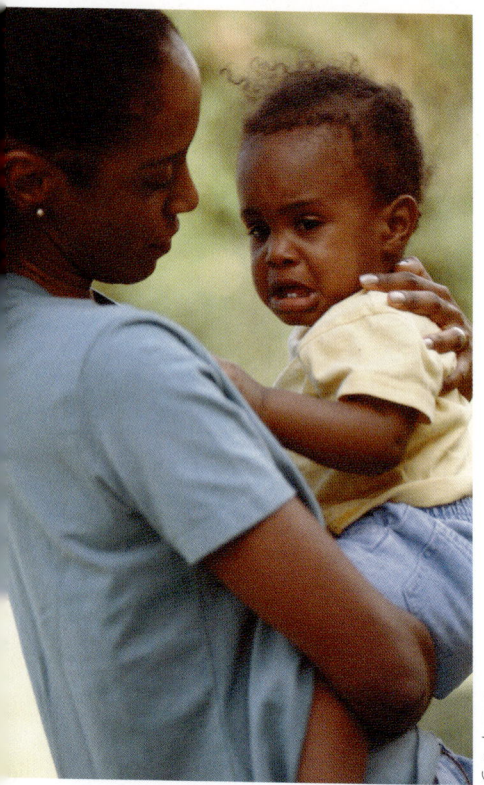

A few children will develop a mild fever, which can be treated with paracetamol. If you suspect other complications see your doctor for reassurance.

NHMRC Australian Standard Vaccination Schedule 2000 (0–4 years)

AGE	VACCINE	
BIRTH	hepB	
2 MONTHS	**OPTION 1**	**OPTION 2**
	DTPa-hepB Hib OPV	DTPa Hib-hepB OPV
4 MONTHS	DTPa-hepB Hib OPV	DTPa Hib-hepB OPV
6 MONTHS	DTPa-hepB OPV	DTPa OPV
12 MONTHS	Hib MMR	MMR Hib-hepB
18 MONTHS	DTPa	
4 YEARS	DTPa MMR OPV	

★ hepB protects against hepatitis B.

★ Hib protects against bacterial meningitis.

★ DTPa (formerly known as triple antigen) protects against diphtheria, tetanus and pertussis (whooping cough).

★ OPV, the oral Sabin vaccine, protects against poliomyelitis.

★ MMR protects against measles, mumps and rubella.

★ The NHMRC 2000 Schedule introduces two options at 2, 4, 6 and 12 months of age, each of which involves the use of a new combination vaccine.

★ Schedule options 1 and 2 may be interchanged with regard to their hepatitis B and Hib components.

★ Hepatitis B vaccine should be given to all infants at birth and should not be delayed beyond 7 days.

★ Wherever possible, use the same brand of DTPa at 2, 4 and 6 months.

common baby ailments

abdominal pain

Tummy pain is a symptom of a number of different conditions. It may simply be caused by colic *(see page 23)*, or be due to constipation *(see page 24)*, to diarrhoea *(see page 26)*, to gastroenteritis *(see page 36)*, to giardiasis *(see page 37)* or even to an intestinal obstruction *(see page 42)*.

Appendicitis is very rare in children under the age of two.

allergies

BABIES CAN DEVELOP ALLERGIES. THE MOST COMMON SITES OF ALLERGIC REACTION ARE:

★ The skin – hives, also known as urticaria *(see page 41)*, and eczema *(see page 31)* are most often seen.

★ Respiratory tract – a runny nose may be allergic rhinitis. Allergy can also cause a cough, even croup *(see page 18)*.

★ Ears *(see page 31)* – may become blocked, resulting in middle ear infection (otitis media).

★ Throat – baby may suffer from a sore throat as the result of the allergy, or from having to breathe through his mouth when he has a blocked nose. Asthma *(see page 13)* and bronchitis *(see page 18)* may also result from allergy.

★ Digestive system – allergy may be caused by an infant formula based on cow's milk (although this is not as common as some people believe). If you suspect allergy is the cause of baby's diarrhoea and vomiting, do not self-diagnose, see your doctor and explain the symptoms. Your baby's diet will need to be supervised by a dietitian. When baby starts eating family foods he may develop a sensitivity to certain foods, but real food allergies are quite rare.

anaemia

Older babies and toddlers quite commonly suffer from anaemia, resulting from a deficiency of iron in the diet. A baby is born with enough stored iron in his body to last six months (unless born prematurely, when baby will already have been prescribed supplements, as premature babies are not born with sufficient stores of iron to last the six months). This is one of the main reasons babies need to start eating family foods at around the six-month mark.

Baby rice cereals fortified with iron, and meat (a natural source of iron), are both important to your baby's diet. It is often one-year-olds on a mainly milk diet who suffer from anaemia. Iron supplements are **not** the answer to this problem as they can cause other problems, including poisoning. An adequate diet is the best preventative. If you are having trouble working out your baby's diet ask your Early Childhood Centre nurse for help, seek out a good book *(see Help on page 60)* or see your family doctor.

antibiotics

Antibiotics kill bacteria. They are useless against viruses. When prescribed and used properly they can be lifesaving, but many health professionals believe we, as a society, are consuming too many of them. If your baby is prescribed antibiotics, make sure that you know when they should be taken (before or after food), and what the possible side-effects are. Always give baby the full course prescribed – do not stop the medicine because you think he looks better. And see your doctor again if you have any concerns.

aspirin

Aspirin has been found to be responsible for the rare but fatal condition Reye's syndrome, and should **never** be given to babies, children or teenagers. Paracetamol is the usual drug given for pain relief in children; it is available in liquid form for babies.

Viktorija Macens

asthma

Asthma affects one in five children, more boys than girls. In fact it is Australia's most common medical condition. Although it is not common in babies under 12 months, if you have a family history of asthma and/or other allergies you need to be aware that an attack of asthma can be triggered by a virus or cigarette smoke, by allergens, pets, house-dust mites or food.

Asthma constricts the bronchial tubes, the airways of the lungs, making breathing difficult. The first sign of asthma is usually a persistent cough, sometimes only at night. Symptoms similar to bronchitis *(see page 18)*, including wheezing, shortness of breath and a tightness in the chest, will follow the cough if it is a symptom of asthma. It is important that you see your doctor if you suspect asthma, or if your baby has an unexplained cough.

bites and stings

animal bites

- Dog bites are among the worst and most common bites a child can suffer. Thousands of children are bitten every year and a considerable percentage are so severely bitten they require reconstructive surgery. The dog most likely to bite is the family pet, or a dog well known to the family. Sudden movements can cause a dog to bite, as can disturbing a sleeping dog, annoying a dog that is eating, and approaching a dog that has been cooped up in a car. Babies who have recently learned to move around, or are just walking, are very vulnerable in these situations. Remember also that dogs that are unfamiliar with small children may be very nervous of them – and a nervous dog is more likely to bite.

- Cat bites are not as common but they can be more dangerous in terms of infection. The risk of infection from a cat bite is high because the bites cause puncture wounds that are not easy to clean. Cat scratches are painful, and can also become infected.

- Wash a bite or scratch very carefully by running it under warm water, and treat with antiseptic. If the wound is large or you are at all worried about it, see your doctor. If any wound caused by an animal becomes infected, red or swollen, see your doctor immediately. Keeping your child's tetanus immunisation up to date is an important precaution (see *Immunisation, page 8*).

insect bites

- Ant, centipede and scorpion bites are all very unpleasant and will upset baby. Applying a cold compress or ice pack, then an anti-itch cream, will soothe.

- Bee stings cause immediate pain and swelling, which worsens over the following 24 hours. Remove the sting by scraping or scooping it away with your fingernail. Do not try to squeeze it out as this releases more venom. Bathe the site and apply ice, unless the sting is close to an eye. Make a paste of soluble aspirin and put it on the sting site to relieve pain. Seek medical help if there is any sign of an allergic reaction such as swelling of the mouth or face, noisy breathing, difficulty swallowing or abnormal drowsiness – these are symptoms of anaphylactic shock and require emergency treatment (see *page 51*).

★ Fleas from animals or birds can bite and may carry disease. If you find fleas on your baby put her – still dressed – in a shallow bath and undress her slowly. You might like to make a game of it. The fleas will jump into the water and drown and you can give your child a proper bath in fresh water and apply an anti-itch cream. Make sure you remove the source of the fleas too, but don't use any strong insecticide near baby's sleeping place.

★ Mosquitoes can carry a number of horrible diseases including Australian encephalitis, Ross River fever and dengue fever, so you do need to try to protect your baby. Electric insect zappers are not hugely successful, however, and long-term use of insect repellents is not advised for babies or young children. Dressing your child in long-sleeved light-coloured clothes (mozzies like dark colours), using mosquito screens on doors and windows, and mosquito nets over cots, are all valuable precautions. Use an anti-itch cream if your child is bitten and be alert for any other symptoms such as a high fever or a rash. If you suspect a complication see your doctor.

★ Spider bites can make a baby seriously ill. The poisonous ones to watch out for particularly are funnel-webs and red-backs. Others which have a nasty bite are wolf spiders, trapdoor spiders, mouse spiders and white-tailed spiders. Never leave clothes and shoes lying on the ground, on the floor in ground-level rooms or in outdoor laundries or sheds. If baby is playing in the garden keep her away from likely spider habitats such as flowerpots, stones and dark places, and watch what she is playing with. If you think your child has been bitten by a spider, seek medical help immediately. Even spiders which are not well known for their venom can cause enormous pain and distress.

★ Ticks burrow into the skin and can make a baby very sick, even cause paralysis. The common hardback tick can cause spotted fever (which may be mistaken for a viral infection). If you find a tick on your baby, flood the site with methylated spirits or mineral turpentine and remove the tick with a pair of tweezers by manoeuvring the points under the tick's swollen body, the object being to remove it in one piece without squeezing it. If baby seems to be in any pain or discomfort take her to the doctor.

For more information about how to manage bites and stings contact the Poisons Information Centre 13 11 26.

 Keep this number by your phone and stored in your mobile phone.

at the beach

Many marine animals are a potential source of danger. It is wise when you are exploring the beach to be cautious yourself and to keep a constant eye on baby. While blue-ringed octopus, box jellyfish and stone-fish are not common, they are a hazard in Australian waters and you need to be aware of their possible presence if you are in an area they inhabit.

taking a temperature

Placing the back of your hand on baby's bare chest is a much better way of telling if your child has a temperature than putting a hand to her forehead. Temperature readings in a child under two years can vary considerably and still be normal. Mouth temperatures can vary from 36.5 to 37.4°C, while rectal temperatures are about half a degree higher. A daily variation of as much as 2°C is quite normal in a baby. A baby's temperature is usually taken by putting a thermometer in her armpit or groin. Ask your Early Childhood Centre nurse to show you how to do it.

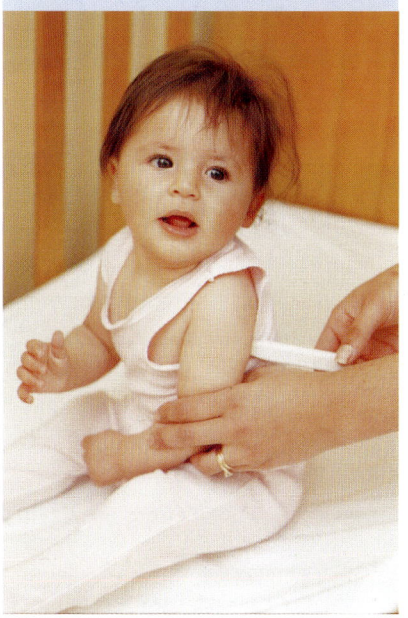

TAKING A TEMPERATURE | 17

breathing problems

It is not unusual for babies to wheeze slightly if they have a minor breathing problem. Noisy breathing, fast breathing, difficult breathing – all are symptoms of a problem. If your baby also has a bluish tinge around the lips or tongue, is unusually drowsy, or seems to be in distress, it is very important that you seek immediate help. Never take chances with your child's breathing.

POSSIBLE CAUSES INCLUDE:

★ Choking – if his breathing difficulties started suddenly, baby may have inhaled some small object. Immediate first aid is important (see page 21). If this is not successful call an ambulance urgently.

★ Asthma – if breathing problems are accompanied by wheezing and coughing at night, baby may have asthma and you need to see your doctor (see page 13).

★ Croup – an acute inflammation of the upper respiratory tract, commonly caused by a virus. When the air passages narrow, breathing becomes noisy and difficult. Inhaling steam can give some relief. Take baby into a warm bathroom and run all the taps, hot and cold, until steam builds up and the coughing ceases. Do not leave baby unattended. In severe attacks croup is a medical emergency.

★ Pneumonia – if your child has had a cold and is lying in bed and breathing fast or seems more ill than is normal with a cold, it could be pneumonia (see page 47). Seek urgent medical help.

bronchiolitis and bronchitis

Bronchiolitis is an inflammation of the bronchioles, the smallest airways in the lungs. It can cause severe breathing difficulties in babies.

Bronchitis is inflammation of the bronchial tubes in the lungs. Symptoms include a dry cough, fever, loss of appetite and noisy breathing.

Both conditions are usually caused by a virus. If you suspect that either of these is the cause of your baby's distress and breathing difficulties, offer plenty of fluids and seek medical attention immediately.

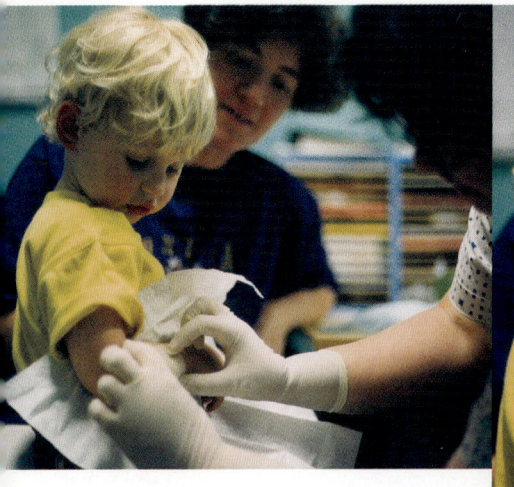
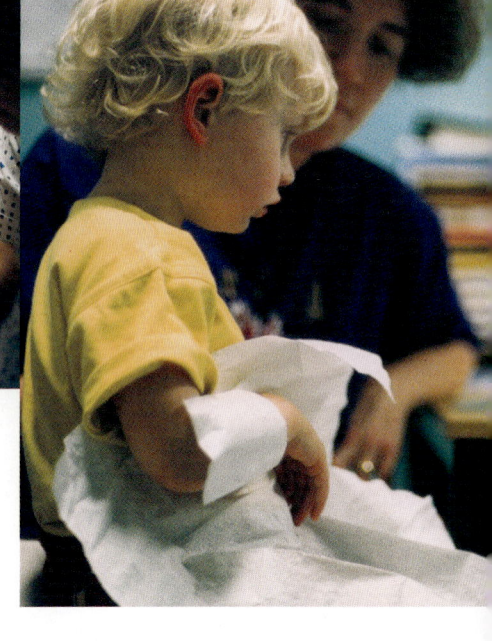

burns and scalds

Burns and scalds are the second most common reason for taking a one-year-old child to casualty (the most common reason is a fall). Burns and scalds most often occur at home, in the kitchen or in the bathroom.

Being aware of the hazards and taking safety measures can minimise the chances of your child becoming a burns victim. Burns are most commonly caused (in order of frequency) by coming in contact with irons, heaters, ovens, part of a lawnmower such as the muffler, hotplates on stoves, cigarettes, hot metals (including saucepans), barbecues and heated floors.

The most common causes of scalds are (in order of frequency) hot drinks such as coffee and tea, hot water from a kettle or mug, hot bathwater and hot foods such as soup. Knowing what to do in case of a burn or scald can make all the difference to the severity of the burn and whether your child will need to be admitted to hospital.

If the child's clothes are on fire you first need to put out the flames. Stop the child, lay him on the floor, wrap him in a coat or blanket to smother the flames and roll him across the ground to put out the fire. For burns or scalds leave the child's clothes on and put him into cool (not cold) water for 30 minutes, making sure he doesn't get cold. Leave the removal of burnt or stuck clothing to medical staff. If you use a wet cloth to cool a burn, rinse it out in fresh cool water every minute. Don't use ice – it can make the burn worse. Seek medical attention urgently.

chickenpox

Also known as varicella, chickenpox is caused by a highly contagious airborne virus. Symptoms are a distinctive itchy rash that quickly turns into blisters, and a slight fever. The disease begins with a mild fever or headache, followed a few hours later by the rash, which occurs mainly on the trunk. Relieving the itch is the most pressing treatment – calamine lotion and oatmeal or bicarbonate of soda baths will often help. Paracetamol is usually given if there is a fever; sometimes antihistamines are given for the itch. It is important that the spots are not scratched as they will leave scars. You may need to put scratch mitts on your baby's hands. The child is infectious until all the scabs have cleared up. Possible complications include a secondary infection from scratching, pneumonia *(see page 47)* and, rarely, encephalitis *(see page 32)*.

choking

While children are learning to chew and before they have their back teeth they are in danger of choking. You can reduce the risk by avoiding hard foods such as raw carrot and apple pieces, cutting meats into small pieces and never giving foods such as nuts, popcorn, corn chips or hard-boiled lollies to children under the age of five. It is also important that a small child sits quietly while eating.

If your child starts to choke on a piece of food don't slap him on the back. If the object is blocking the airway you have an emergency and need to seek medical help immediately. He may turn red then blue or he may try to cry but make no noise. If he stops breathing and becomes unconscious, sit down and place baby across your lap, face downwards. Give two blows to his back with the heel of your hand between the shoulder blades. If you are familiar with **Expired Air Resuscitation** techniques, now may be the time to use them. Keep doing the EAR until help comes or you free the object. Do not put your fingers down a child's throat unless the object is clearly visible. The emergency number in Australia is **000** – write this up next to your telephone.

CHOKING 21

coeliac disease

This condition occurs when the digestive system cannot deal with the types of grain which contain gluten. The main symptoms are persistent bouts of diarrhoea and a failure to gain weight.

Seek medical attention if you suspect your baby has this problem.

Treatment is to remove the offending grains, notably wheat, rye, barley and oats, from the diet for life. This must be done only under medical supervision.

colds

Colds are caused by viral infections of the upper respiratory tract. Babies and toddlers with older siblings get many colds (an average of eight a year). A runny nose, sometimes a sore throat, muscle pains, aches, a mild fever and headaches are typical symptoms. Colds are transmitted by the inhalation of infected airborne particles. In new babies colds are generally mild but a stuffy nose can be very distressing if it prevents easy breathing and the ability to suck. You may have to use saline drops to clear baby's nose. Some mothers swear by a drop or two of breast milk to dry up the mucus before breastfeeding. Do not give your child any over-the-counter cold medicines, or nasal sprays or drops, without first consulting your doctor. You can give paracetamol to reduce a fever, and encourage baby to drink plenty of fluids. If there is no improvement within 48 hours, see your doctor.

colic

Colic is common between the ages of one and 16 weeks. It has been defined as attacks of excessive crying, or crying for at least three hours a day, three days a week. The cause may be too much wind in the intestine, or a reaction to infant formula or to some substance that has crossed over into the breast milk. Some even believe colic is the result of parental tension. It's serious when your baby is crying for hour upon hour and appears to be in distress. Before you take her to the doctor, try checking whether she is hungry, and try once more to put her to sleep – even if you have to take her for a walk in her stroller or her sling, or for a ride in the car in the middle of the night.

(See also Abdominal pain, page 10, Intestinal obstruction, page 42.)

concussion

See Head injuries, page 38.

conjunctivitis

This is an infection of the membranes lining the eyelid and/or covering the white of the eye. The sticky, crusty discharge is highly contagious and can spread the condition to adults. It is important to visit your doctor as antibiotic drops may be necessary. You need to be scrupulously careful about washing your baby's face and eyes, using only fresh cotton wool balls.

(See also Eye problems, page 32.)

constipation

Breastfed babies are rarely constipated, but babies who are fed infant formula and those who have begun to eat family foods can be. Some breastfed babies may not have a motion for days and still not be constipated, others may have up to eight a day. As babies get older they pass fewer motions and by the age of four months the average is two per day. Hard motions which cause discomfort indicate constipation. They suggest that your child needs more fibre in her diet – plenty of fruit, vegetables and wholemeal cereals. Bran is not suitable as it can interfere with the absorption of vitamins and minerals. Check that baby is getting enough fluids – she should have seven or more wet nappies in a 24-hour period. Check that you are making up the infant formula strictly according to the directions on the container. Offer a bottle-fed baby extra cool boiled water – don't dilute the formula.
For babies over four months, between 30 and 120ml of prune juice may solve the problem. If it does not, take her to the doctor.

convulsions

Convulsions can occur in babies and young children in association with infection and a high fever (febrile convulsions), and are very frightening for parents. There is little that can be done while a convulsion takes place, except to watch and be sure your child is safe. When it is over, seek medical advice. Most children who suffer a febrile convulsion (often called a fit) will only ever have one. The tendency to suffer such fits seems to run in families.

coughs

See Breathing problems, page 18, Bronchiolitis and bronchitis, page 18, Pneumonia, page 47, Whooping cough, page 57.

cradle cap

A skin condition caused when sebum, secreted from the sebaceous glands in the skin, forms crusty layers on the scalp. Though it looks dirty it is not. Treatment is to gently rub olive oil into the crusts (even those on baby's soft spot or fontanelle), and next day wash with soap and warm water. This procedure may have to be repeated for several nights until the crusts disappear.

croup

See Breathing problems, page 18.

dehydration

The result of depletion of the body's water content, this is a life-threatening condition, particularly in babies, whose bodies require more fluid relative to body weight than adults' bodies do. They also use up the water in their bodies more rapidly than adults.

Dehydration can occur as a result of heat stroke or heat exhaustion, or diarrhoea and vomiting. The child will become apathetic, his eyes and the fontanelle (soft spot) will look sunken, the mouth will be dry and nappies will be wet infrequently. Normal skin springs back into place when gently pinched; dehydrated skin stays in the pinch. Urgent medical attention is vital.

diarrhoea

Getty Images

Loose, pasty motions are normal in breastfed babies, who seldom contract infectious diarrhoea. Babies who are being given soy milk infant formula will also have slightly loose motions. Babies who are bottle-fed are more susceptible to diarrhoea. As the growing child begins to put anything and everything into his mouth and begins to eat family foods he has a greater chance of contracting viral or bacterial diarrhoea infections. Diarrhoea is very smelly, greenish, watery and awfully messy, often expelled explosively in large amounts. If diarrhoea persists for a day or more, seek medical attention. If baby is vomiting as well, it is urgent that you seek medical attention.

Diarrhoea is very different from a normal bowel motion.

The treatment will depend on the doctor's diagnosis.

Modifying baby's diet, changing his formula or using over-the-counter remedies may worsen the situation. Being scrupulously clean and keeping baby isolated may prevent the infection spreading to other children.

(See also Giardiasis, page 37, Vomiting, page 56.)

DIARRHOEA 27

dislocation

A dislocation occurs when the bones of a joint are pushed out of contact with each other because the ligaments have been stretched or torn. About one baby in 1000 has congenital hip dislocation at birth. All newborn babies are screened for this condition, the causes of which are not known. If it does not correct itself in the first two weeks, baby may need to wear a special splint for two to four months.

The most common dislocation seen in small children as the result of an accident is the elbow, sometimes called "pulled elbow". Medical treatment is necessary, usually an X-ray followed by an anaesthetic while the bones are manipulated back into position. Dislocations usually heal within a week or two.

diphtheria

Fortunately now rare because of immunisation *(see page 8)*, diphtheria is a highly contagious disease which begins with a sore throat and can lead to a blockage of the respiratory tract and serious complications. Urgent medical attention is essential if you suspect baby has this disease.

drowning

The high number of children in the under-four age group who drown each year is a national tragedy. Babies can, and do, drown in just a few centimetres of water — in bathtubs, nappy buckets, swimming pools and irrigation canals.

A baby can slide almost silently under water or fall in while an adult's back is momentarily turned.

Prevention is all-important. Nappy buckets must be kept away from children (in laundry tubs) and must have tight-fitting lids. Swimming pools should be fenced and have safety gates; farm gates giving access to creeks and dams must be kept closed; bath-time must always be supervised.

Parents need to be constantly aware near any water. If your child should fall into water it is important to get him out as quickly as possible and lay him on his side. If he is not breathing call for help and begin resuscitation immediately.

Very young children can be taught water familiarisation and enjoy "swimming" with adults, but this will not prevent drowning.

ear problems

Ear problems are common in small children. Babies are particularly susceptible to inflammation of the middle ear (otitis media) because they spend much of their time lying down and their eustachian tubes, which connect the middle ear to the throat, are shorter and straighter than in older children, thus making it easier for bacteria, often from an infection associated with a cold, to enter.

Ear pain will cause a baby to cry, or even scream, and pull or tug his ear if the pain is severe. Fever, vomiting and loss of appetite can accompany ear pain. A visit to the doctor is important and antibiotics and pain relief are likely to be prescribed. Babies can also suffer from excess wax which collects in the outer ear and may need to be removed, but first check with your doctor.

Older babies are also quite capable of poking small objects into their ears. If the offending item is not easy to remove, take your child to the doctor. A baby who is born with a hearing deficit will respond normally for the first few months, but around six months will stop babbling. If you think your baby is not hearing or listening, seek medical advice and ask for a hearing test to be done.

(See also Teething, page 52.)

eczema

Eczema, which often occurs in families, is an itchy skin condition with bright red, scaly patches, usually beginning on a baby's cheeks and forehead. Toddlers who suffer from eczema will have patches of it on the creases of knees, elbows and ankles, and inside the wrists. When affected areas are scratched they weep clear fluid, which forms crusts.

Very few people have eczema caused by an allergy. Total breastfeeding for at least five months can delay the onset of eczema in a child whose family has a history of this condition. When baby starts eating family foods, some foods, such as cow's milk protein and wheat, may make the condition worse. Certain things can further irritate the skin, including wool fabrics, perfumed products, detergent, chlorine and rapid changes in temperature.

Treatment is usually with moisturisers such as sorbolene cream with 10 per cent glycerine. Cortisone cream may be prescribed for severe conditions.

Mild eczema and skin rashes are common on babies' young vulnerable skin.

encephalitis

In newborn babies, the herpes simplex virus is the most common cause of encephalitis, which is an inflammation of the brain.

It is a rare condition; symptoms include abnormal drowsiness, fever, irritability, vomiting, weakness of a limb or limbs, and convulsions. Medical care is vital and will include a brain scan. Most children recover completely.

eye problems

Babies are susceptible to problems such as blocked tear ducts and conjunctivitis *(see page 23)*. Your doctor will show you how to treat both conditions – blocked tear ducts will require massage and conjunctivitis will need treatment with antibiotics.

Newborns may squint until the age of two to four months. It is not true that babies are unable to see clearly. Healthy newborn babies will focus on the faces of their parents within minutes of birth and can see clearly to a distance of about 25cm. By four months of age, they will be able to focus and reach for toys and other objects which are held close to them.

Viktorija Macens

One of the most common eye problems in children is strabismus (also known as "cross eyes" or "lazy eyes"), which may be present at birth or appear later. Children do **not** outgrow this condition and it needs immediate treatment by an ophthalmologist to prevent sight problems developing.

Always seek immediate medical advice if you have any concerns about your child's eyes.

fever

Fever or high temperature is a defect in control of body temperature. Babies from the age of around six weeks to 12 months can get a fever from respiratory infections, tonsillitis, ear infections or immunisations. Your baby will be unhappy, flushed and feel hot to the touch. Taking baby's temperature will confirm your fears *(see page 17)*. It is important to consult a doctor if your baby has a high temperature as it could be caused by one of many diseases or conditions.

A high temperature in babies and young children can cause febrile convulsions *(see Convulsions, page 24, Taking a temperature, page 17)*.

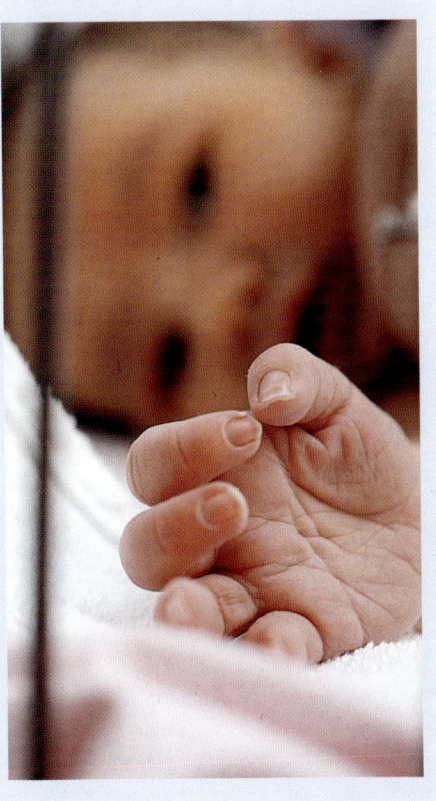

finger injuries

Little fingers get poked and stuck in the most extraordinary places, but one of the most common causes of finger injury is confrontation with a door. It is very easy to trap a little finger in the edge of a door – and wooden doors can do just as much damage as car doors. A fracture or even amputation can be the result of entrapment. If baby's finger or hand is injured, control any bleeding, immobilise the hand and seek immediate medical attention.

foot problems

Little feet and ankles may be cramped and turned in at birth, but during the first month a baby's feet will usually straighten out. The arch of a baby's foot is padded with a layer of fat to prevent heat loss, which gives a flat-footed appearance. Many babies have a toe overlapping or underlapping another. Curly or bent toes and flat feet rarely cause a problem. Pigeon toes refers to feet which turn in as the child walks. It may be caused by a twist in one of the leg bones and will usually correct itself in time. Braces or special shoes are not needed. Babies born with club foot or metatarsus varus (foot angled from the instep) require treatment and you will need to consult a paediatrician. Babies need to learn to walk in bare feet. They do not need shoes until they are walking about in public places. Putting shoes on early walkers reduces their mobility and can slow down the development of their walking skills.

fractures

A broken bone in a very young child is most likely to be a greenstick (or partial) fracture of the leg or arm, or of the collarbone. A broken bone will result in symptoms which may include severe pain, extreme tenderness near the site of the fracture, swelling and skin discolouration. A serious fracture will result in an obvious deformity. If you suspect a fracture, control any bleeding, protect and immobilise the area – a thick newspaper makes a good temporary splint – then transport the child to the doctor or hospital casualty. An X-ray will confirm the fracture. A fractured limb will probably be put in a plaster cast, although in some cases metal screws and rods are inserted. Fractures in children heal much faster than in adults – a finger may take only a week.

Doors, even wooden ones, are a common cause of finger injuries in little explorers.

gastric reflux

The full name of this condition, thought to be caused by an immature valve between the oesophagus and the stomach, is gastro-oesophageal reflux. Reflux is characterised by true vomiting (not simple possetting), which can cause pain and make a baby very unsettled. It is also upsetting for parents who have to cope regularly with regurgitated feeds and mess and an unhappy baby. The vomiting of reflux can happen any time, though it is more likely after a feed. Baby may even refuse to feed because he associates it with pain. Lying down can make it worse and make baby more irritable. Feeding baby small and frequent feeds in a semi-upright position often helps, as can sitting him in a baby chair or putting him in a sling after the feed. Baby may also prefer to sleep with the mattress in a slightly tilted position.

Many sufferers grow out of gastric reflux by their first birthday, but others take much longer. Medications are available from your doctor to help with this condition. Sometimes bottle-feeding with specially thickened formula is recommended, though there is some doubt as to how useful this is.

gastroenteritis

This is a very serious illness in babies and young children because it can cause them to dehydrate very quickly. It requires urgent medical attention.

Symptoms include vomiting, diarrhoea, abdominal cramps, loss of appetite and possibly fever. Vomiting is usually the first symptom, followed by watery abnormal diarrhoea, which can persist for a week or longer.

Gastroenteritis is usually caused by a virus, although bacteria, often from contaminated food, can also be responsible. Poor hygiene is commonly the reason for the infection. Keeping your baby away from children with gastroenteritis, together with observing good hygiene, are the best precautions.

Fluid intake during a bout of gastroenteritis is very important. Breastfed babies will need plenty of feeds, together with extra boiled water. The best fluid to give a child who is eating family foods is water with a mixture of special salts, known as electrolyte replacers, available from pharmacies. Never give lemonade or fruit juice and never give medication to prevent vomiting or diarrhoea except under your doctor's advice.

In a baby under three months of age, gastroenteritis is a medical emergency. For older babies, medical attention is also the wisest course.

(See also Dehydration, page 26, Diarrhoea, page 26, Vomiting, page 56.)

genital problems

★ Boys – pain or swelling in the scrotum may mean an inguinal hernia or hydrocele, or possibly an injury; pain with discharge from the penis may be balanitis; pain on passing urine is likely to be a urinary tract infection. All these conditions require urgent medical attention.

★ Girls – itching and inflammation of the genitals is the most common genital problem. It is caused by vulvovaginitis, and medical attention is needed.

german measles

See Rubella, page 50.

giardiasis

The bowel infection giardiasis is caused by a small organism found in contaminated water. It can come from water left in wading pools, or from puddles lying in the backyard. Babies on the move are quite susceptible.

Symptoms are large frothy smelly stools – often with stomach cramps – and a stool sample is usually taken for diagnosis. A course of antibiotics normally cures the problem quickly.

head injuries

Bangs to the head are quite common childhood injuries, often from falling out of a cot, off a change table or down stairs. While injuries to the head often bleed profusely, the main risk is internal bleeding. In most cases a bump or swelling will be the only symptom; however, if the child has briefly lost consciousness he may have concussion and should be seen by a doctor. If he appears confused or drowsy, vomits persistently or has blood coming from the nose or ears, urgent medical attention is essential. X-rays will be taken and a CT scan may be performed to check for brain haemorrhage. Any time your child falls on his head, a medical checkup is the wisest precaution.

heart murmurs

Heart murmurs are extra noises made by the heart, usually detected during a routine medical checkup. They do not necessarily indicate abnormality. Many such sounds will disappear by the time the child reaches adolescence. Regular checkups for a child with a heart murmur are a wise precaution.

heat problems

Over-exposure to heat can cause heat exhaustion or heat stroke. Heat exhaustion occurs when an excessive amount of the body's fluid is lost. Babies and small children are particularly susceptible (see Dehydration, page 26). Children who are left in a car, even on a day that doesn't seem excessively hot, are at risk of overheating very quickly. This can result in heat stroke, which is a medical emergency. The child's temperature will be as high as 40°C and he will look flushed, though his skin will be dry. There will be a racing pulse and breathing may be noisy. He may lose consciousness. Treatment aims to reduce the child's temperature as quickly as possible and restore the body's fluids. Urgent medical attention is essential. In the meantime, remove the child's clothes, lay him in the shade with his feet higher than his head and wrap him in something wet such as a towel. If he is unconscious place him on his side.

Leaving a child unattended in a car at any time can result in heavy penalties.

Caused by perspiration, heat rash (prickly heat) is a rash consisting of itchy red spots and very small blisters that appears in hot weather. Keeping baby cool will help the rash to disappear and prevent its return.

hepatitis

The liver infections hepatitis B and hepatitis C can be transmitted to newborn babies by mothers who are carriers of the viruses. Hepatitis B, which destroys the liver, is a serious, even fatal, illness that is currently incurable. Hepatitis C, which is potentially more dangerous, is mostly seen in intravenous drug users. The current immunisation schedule recommends that all babies be vaccinated at birth against hepatitis B.

hernia

A hernia occurs when part of the intestine protrudes through the muscles of the intestinal wall. The most common types in children are umbilical hernia, when the intestine bulges through the muscle wall at or above the navel; and inguinal hernia, when the intestine protrudes into the inguinal canal in the groin. Umbilical hernias are usually uncomplicated and disappear of their own accord; if there is no improvement by the age of five, an operation may be necessary.

There's always plenty of activity at Admissions in a city children's hospital.

Inguinal hernias can be dangerous, as they occur when the inguinal canal, which normally closes shortly after birth, remains open and leaves a space through which a loop of intestine can pass into the groin or scrotum. These hernias do not disappear without treatment, and surgery is necessary.

HIV infection and AIDS

Most babies who are affected by HIV (human immunodeficiency virus) have contracted it from their infected mother around the time of birth. Medical supervision is essential for a child with HIV.

hives

The medical term for hives is urticaria. Hives may appear as itchy white lumps on a red base or as weals, sometimes quite extensive, on body and limbs. They are likely to be an allergic reaction to a specific food such as citrus or milk, to a medicine such as penicillin, or an insect or plant sting. A doctor may prescribe antihistamines to relieve the symptoms, and a soothing lotion will help in most cases. Severe cases may need oral corticosteroids.

immunisation

See page 8.

impetigo

Also known as "school sores", but common in babies, impetigo most commonly affects the mouth and nose area and the nappy area, but can appear anywhere on the body. Caused by bacteria which enters the skin through a cut, insect bite or skin condition such as eczema, impetigo begins as small blisters. The blisters burst to form large crusts which are highly contagious. Bedding and clothing need to be washed every day and the infected baby needs to be kept away from others.

With treatment, usually an antibiotic ointment, the sores generally clear up in five days.

influenza

Caused by viruses that are ever-changing, true influenza is highly contagious and occurs in epidemics. It is transmitted by sneezing and coughing, when droplets from the nose and throat of an infected person pass to others.

Incubation is between one and three days and sufferers are usually contagious before they know they have the illness. Symptoms include fever, dry cough, muscular aches, stuffy nose, tiredness and weakness, headache and sometimes a sore throat.

Seek medical attention if your baby contracts influenza, as her temperature and tendency to dehydrate will need to be monitored.

(See also Fever, page 33, Gastroenteritis, page 36.)

insect bites and stings

See Bites and stings, page 14.

intestinal obstruction

When the small or large intestine is blocked or partially blocked, it is known as an intestinal obstruction.

Intussusception (when one part of the intestine slips into another) is rare and the usual cause of intestinal obstruction in babies under 12 months – it requires urgent medical attention. The symptoms resemble severe colic. Baby will be in severe pain, drawing her little legs up to her chest and screaming. She may vomit and may also pass a stool with blood in it.

Early diagnosis is critical and you need to seek help immediately. The child may have an X-ray and possibly surgery.

A strangulated hernia can also cause a blocked intestine in babies, while pyloric stenosis is a partial blockage that occurs in babies under the age of two months. It requires urgent medical attention and possible surgery.

(See also Abdominal pain, page 10.)

lead poisoning

See Pollution effects, page 49.

Viktorija Macens

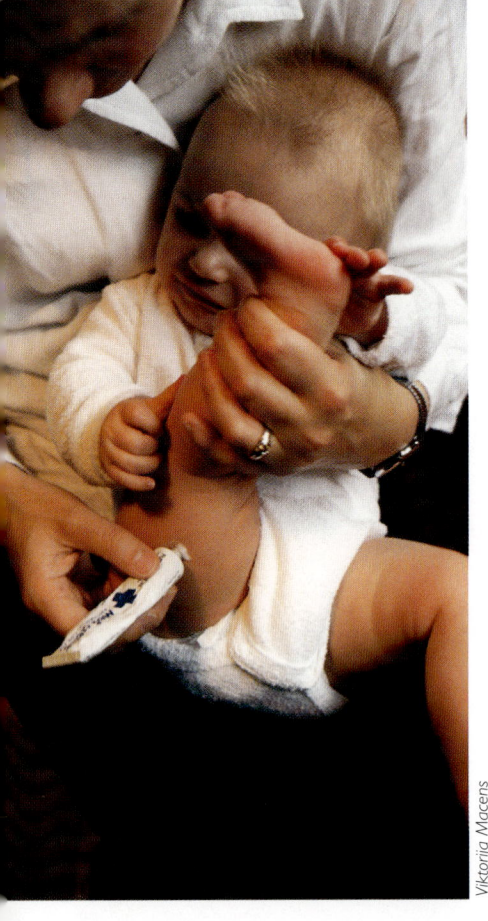

leg problems

Bow-legs and knock-knees are common in the under-twos. Bowing is caused in the womb if the soft bones of the legs are constricted. Bow-legs, which can cause the child to walk pigeon-toed, are usually self-correcting. Knock-knees do not show up until around 18 months, and also usually correct themselves. Seek medical advice rather than making your own diagnosis.

lumps and swellings

These may be caused by swollen glands, insect bites or injuries. Any lump or swelling which is persistent, or whose cause is not obvious, needs to be checked by a doctor.

(See also Bites and stings, page 14, Mumps, page 47, Roseola infantum, page 50, Rubella, page 50.)

Viktorija Macens

measles

The dangerous thing about measles is not the illness itself (which is caused by a virus), but the slight possibility of serious complications. Measles can occasionally cause encephalitis (see page 32) which is a serious, sometimes fatal, condition. Several years after an attack of measles, the rare but fatal degenerative condition known as subacute sclerosing panencephalitis (SSPE) can develop.

These complications are the reason immunisation against measles is important. Measles is spread via secretions from the infected person's nose and mouth. It starts with a runny nose, a dry cough and headache. A high fever and watery eyes precede the rash, which begins as tiny white spots with a red base (Koplik's spots) followed by a flat red blotchy rash appearing first on the face and behind the ears, and later over the whole body. This lasts three or four days before fading.

If you suspect measles you need to take your child to the doctor within 24 hours. Most children recover completely.

meningitis

This is a life-threatening infection of the membranes (meninges) lining the brain and the spinal cord. It can be caused by infection with bacteria or viruses. Though the symptoms may be mild, bacterial meningitis, which is most common in children under the age of five years, can be life-threatening. One type of bacteria that causes it normally lives in the nose and throat, causing no ill effects, but for some unknown reason sometimes travelling to the brain and causing meningococcal meningitis.

The bacterium *Haemophilus influenzae* can also cause meningitis, but since immunisation against Hib was included in the immunisation schedule, it has become less common. Symptoms include abnormal drowsiness, fever, vomiting, refusing food, a bulging fontanelle, inability to tolerate bright lights and occasionally a purple rash. Meningitis is an emergency and if you suspect your child may have this infection urgent medical attention is vital.

High-dose antibiotics will be given immediately for bacterial meningitis and intravenous fluids and anticonvulsants may also be necessary. Prompt treatment usually leads to complete recovery. If treatment is delayed, brain damage may result. Viral meningitis occurs mostly in children over five.

milia

See Rashes, page 50.

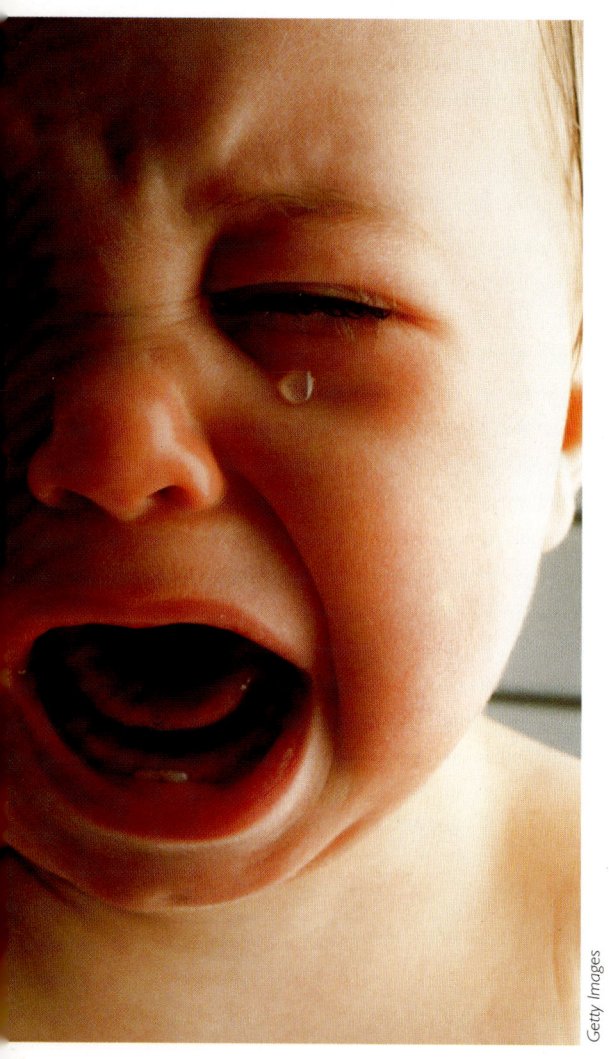

mouth problems

Your baby's mouth is a very important tool – not only for eating and drinking and talking but also for exploring the world around him. The mouth can be easily damaged. Even primary teeth need good care because they are important to the growth and development of the mouth and secondary teeth. Ulcers may develop for no obvious reason, and they tend to recur. They can make your baby's mouth quite painful, but they are not serious and will usually heal on their own. Dental caries (or tooth decay) can occur very early on if baby is regularly allowed to fall asleep while sucking on a bottle of milk, if his dummy is coated with sweet things such as honey or sweetened condensed milk, if he is given unsuitable drinks such as cola, or if his teeth are not cared for. It is important to clean baby's teeth daily from the time they first appear and to take him for a dental checkup around his first birthday.

Oral thrush is a mouth infection quite often seen in babies *(see page 54)*. *(See also Teething, page 52.)*

mumps

Mumps usually affect children aged five to 15, but can affect children of any age. The symptoms can appear up to 21 days after contact with the infection and include fever, and pain around the ears. Quite often the sudden appearance of marked swelling below and in front of one or both ears is the first sign. Mumps can lead to serious complications, including meningitis, pancreatitis and deafness. This disease can be prevented with immunisation *(see page 8)*. If you suspect your baby has mumps you need to take him to the doctor.

nose problems

It is not unusual for a baby to be born with a squashed nose, which usually fills out in the first few days. The most common cause of nose problems is the common cold *(see page 23)*. However, it is also quite common for small objects to be poked up little noses. If you suspect this has happened (an unpleasant discharge may be the only indicator), do not attempt to remove it – your child needs to see a doctor.

pertussis

See *Whooping cough, page 57.*

pigeon toes

See *Foot problems, page 34.*

pneumonia

Pneumonia is an infection of the lungs which can be caused by either bacteria or viruses. It may be a complication of an upper respiratory tract infection such as a cold *(see page 23)*, or of a more serious infectious disease, such as chickenpox *(page 21)* or whooping cough *(page 57)*.

A baby with pneumonia will have a high fever and his breathing will be rapid. He may have a dry cough and chest pain, and may also vomit and suffer from diarrhoea.

Pneumonia is a serious illness and needs medical attention.

poisoning

Any substance that can cause illness or death is a poison. The most common substance swallowed in poisonous amounts by children under the age of three is paracetamol. Other poisonous substances swallowed by young children include medicines for respiratory problems, caustics such as dishwasher detergents, beta blockers (for heart treatment), horticultural and herbal mixtures, eucalyptus oil, antibiotics, anti-inflammatory and anti-histamine drugs, iron supplements, alcohol, rat and insect repellents, turpentine and kerosene, camphor and tobacco.

It is important to keep all medications and household cleaning products in locked cupboards or on high shelves. Alcohol, tobacco, iron supplements and any other substances which are dangerous to young children must be kept locked away as well. It is important too, that visitors' handbags be kept away from mobile and inquisitive little people.

Symptoms of poisoning can include rapid breathing, nausea, over-excitement, vomiting and unconsciousness. The lips, mouth and throat will be burned if an acid or alkali has been swallowed.

Poisons Information Centre: 13 11 26.

Keep this number next to your telephone and stored in your mobile phone. Call for help immediately if your baby swallows anything suspicious or unusual. Never induce vomiting unless instructed to do so.

(See also Bites and stings, page 14, Gastroenteritis, page 36, Pollution, page 49.)

poliomyelitis

Poliomyelitis is a disease caused by a virus that penetrates tissues of the central nervous system, causing paralysis usually beginning in the legs. It has been completely wiped out in Australia by the immunisation program which includes the Sabin vaccine against polio.

pollution effects

★ Lead pollution is a major health hazard for children under four years of age because exposure to lead affects intellectual development adversely – and often permanently. Children most likely to be affected are those aged between nine months and four years who live close to major lead industries, and those living in older houses that have peeling paint or are being renovated. Lead in soil and household dust are the major sources of the pollution. Another major cause of lead contamination in children is lead in petrol, one reason why unleaded petrol is so important. If you think your child is at risk, ask your doctor to test his blood lead level. Chelation therapy may be used to hasten excretion of high levels of lead from the body. The risk of lead pollution can be minimised by keeping your child away from old houses that are being renovated or, if you live in a contaminated area, being scrupulous about cleaning. Floors need to be washed at least twice a month and furniture wiped over fortnightly. Vacuuming, not sweeping, is important. Grass and paving can be laid to cover any exposed soil. Regularly washing hands, all fruits and vegetables, and pets, also helps.

★ Other pollutants which may affect your child include pesticides – both household and agricultural types – and industrial chemicals in the environment. Having your house fumigated for termites or other insects, and using insect "bombs", can leave toxic chemicals in your child's environment. If you must use these pesticides, ensure that your child is kept away from the house for a few days to limit the risk of poisoning.

rashes

Baby's soft tender skin is very susceptible to rashes – which can be caused by allergies, viruses, bites, stings or an illness. If a rash worries you, take baby to the doctor – and when you make the appointment advise them that baby has a rash. They may wish to schedule the appointment to avoid pregnant patients coming in contact with an infectious illness such as rubella *(see below)*. Newborn babies can develop rashes such as heat rash and hives. They may also develop a harmless rash known as toxic erythema (or erythema toxicum), red spots with fluid-filled centres that appear mainly on the trunk and limbs and disappear a few days later of their own accord. Milia are harmless small white spots that appear mostly on the bridge of the nose, and other parts of the face. Caused by temporary blockages in the sebaceous glands of the skin, these too will disappear of their own accord.

(See also Chickenpox, page 21, Eczema, page 31, Heat problems, page 39, Hives, page 41, Measles, page 44, Meningitis, page 44, Roseola infantum, page 50, Rubella, page 50, Scabies, page 51, Scarlet fever, page 51.)

roseola infantum

Common, but not very well known, this rash produces a high fever for about three days which can trigger convulsions. As the fever fades, small, sometimes bumpy, pink spots appear all over the body and may last about 24 hours.

Some children also suffer from mild diarrhoea, a cough, enlarged lymph nodes in the neck and earache and upper eyelid swelling. Keeping the fever down by sponging your child with cool, not cold, water will help and possibly prevent convulsions. A visit to the doctor will rule out any other diseases and reassure you, but do advise your doctor of the rash in case it is rubella *(see below)*. Recovery is usually rapid and the child feels better once the rash has disappeared.

rubella

This mild viral infection, also known as German measles, can cause serious damage to a developing foetus during pregnancy. If you suspect that baby has rubella, take him to the doctor – and when you make the appointment advise them of your suspicions. They may wish to schedule the appointment to avoid the risk of pregnant patients coming in contact with the disease. The symptoms can include a rash, swelling of the lymph nodes and a slight fever, although in a quarter of cases no rash will appear and there is no apparent indication that the baby has the disease. You may need to give your child paracetamol to bring down the fever – and plenty of fluids. It is important to prevent your child coming in contact with any woman who is planning to be, or thinks she might be, pregnant. Rubella is infectious for one week after the rash appears.

scabies

A tiny mite that burrows into the skin to lay its eggs, but lives and breeds on the surface, causes the itch of scabies. Scabies is highly contagious, and passes from person to person by bodily contact. Scabies first appears as a rash of small blisters or pimples, often in the soft creases of the skin. Treatment is a cream or lotion which has to be applied to all areas of the body and then washed off after 24 hours. The mites usually die within three days.

scarlet fever

Now rare because of antibiotics, scarlet fever is a bacterial throat infection that causes a rash, vomiting, sore throat and headache, flushed cheeks and a thick white coating on the tongue. Possible complications of scarlet fever include rheumatic fever. Take baby to the doctor immediately if you suspect this illness.

shock

It is important to take clinical shock seriously, as it can be fatal – at any age. Shock usually occurs after severe bleeding or other loss of body fluid. Symptoms include weakness, a rapid pulse, paleness, cold and clammy skin, chills, a dry mouth, nausea, rapid shallow breathing, restlessness and confusion. Medical attention is required.

Anaphylactic shock, which is fortunately rare, is a severe allergic reaction to certain insect stings, medicines or foods, and requires urgent medical attention, as it can be fatal. Keep your child warm and in a semi-sitting position while you wait for the ambulance.

sneezing

Sneezing is common in young babies and may mean nothing. It may also be a symptom of a cold *(see page 23)* or influenza *(see page 42)*.

splinters

As babies start to move about they quite commonly pick up splinters in their hands, elbows, knees and toes. For tiny splinters that you can hardly see you can use warm wax (not hot) on the spot. Once the wax has set, removing it will pull out the splinter. Chances are, however, that you will have to use a good pair of tweezers, a needle and a steady hand. You'll need plenty of light and if possible another person to hold and comfort your child. Large splinters will need medical attention.

suffocation

A baby can suffocate in a plastic bag, a swimming cap, a pillow, on a sofa or by getting stuck in the corner of a pram or bed. The most important thing is to restore the supply of air as quickly as possible by removing any obstruction and immediately starting resuscitation if breathing has stopped. An ambulance must be called.

sunburn

Baby's skin is too delicate to be exposed to the sun. In summer babies need to be kept out of the sun between the hours of 11am and 3pm, Standard Time. When you are outdoors with baby, dress her in long-sleeved tops and a hat. In summer, or in any warm weather, apply a sunscreen designed for babies.

At the beach be sure you have at least one sunshade, and "set up camp" in a shady place out of the wind. When baby is in the water, she should wear a protective swimsuit and hat, as well as sunscreen on all exposed skin. If she should suffer sunburn, cool her skin with cool water and give her plenty of fluids, including boiled water. If there is any blistering, seek medical attention.

teething

A baby's first tooth can arrive at any time between the ages of three and 13 months, and usually starts with a small, pale bump on the lower gum. Common signs are dribbling, sore gums and lots of chewing. Diarrhoea, fever, vomiting and convulsions are **not** symptoms of teething – they are symptoms of sickness.

Babies often tug at their ears when they are teething, not because they have earache but because the teeth are hurting as they come through – the lower jaw and teeth share the same nerve as the ear canal so baby feels soreness in her ear. Abscesses are possible, so if baby's tooth is surrounded by red, angry-looking skin have it checked out by your doctor or dentist.

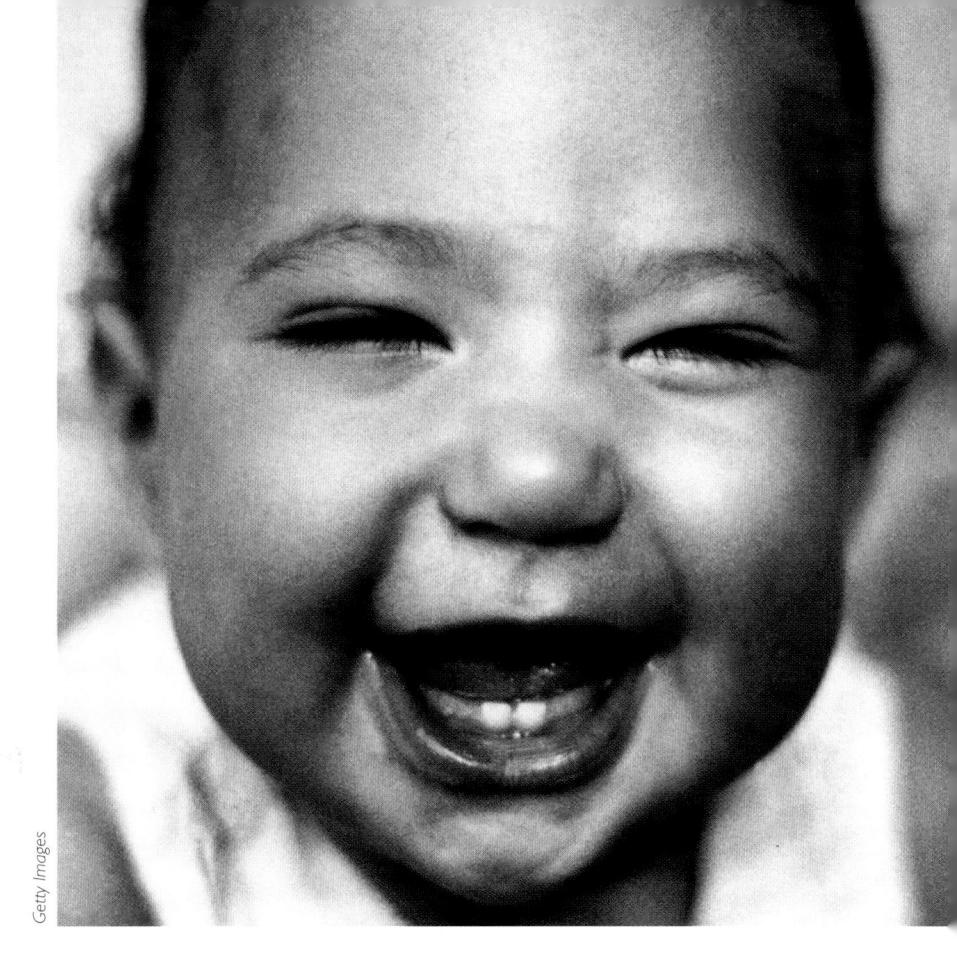

As soon as baby's first teeth appear it is important to start cleaning them.

You don't need a toothbrush to begin with; a clean face washer is ideal. Sit baby on your lap facing away from you and gently clean around the tooth or teeth with the washer. As more teeth appear you might like to buy a first toothbrush, which is more like a gum massager, and later a soft baby toothbrush.

(See also Mouth problems, page 46).

tetanus

A serious disease produced by bacteria entering the body through a dirty wound, tetanus is now rare amongst children in developed countries because of immunisation and is more likely to occur in older persons whose immunisation is no longer effective. The mostly likely source is garden soil contaminated by animal manure. Tetanus was once called "lockjaw", because one of the symptoms is an inability to open the mouth. Other symptoms are difficulty in swallowing, contraction of facial muscles and spasms of muscles in the neck, back and abdomen.

Tetanus is a medical emergency and will require admission to hospital. It is easily prevented by immunisation.

threadworms

See Worms, page 58.

thrush

Oral thrush is an infection caused by abnormal growth of the yeast *Candida albicans*, occurring most commonly in babies under 12 months of age. The symptoms are a sore mouth, and yellow-white spots on the tongue and inside the mouth. Antifungal gel or drops prescribed by a doctor are the usual treatment. If you are breastfeeding you may also need to use this medication on your nipples. If you are bottle-feeding, sterilising will need to be meticulous.

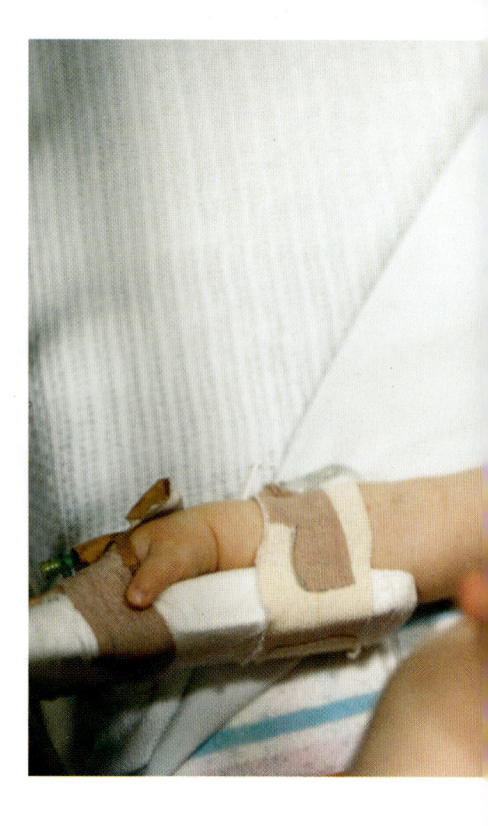

An intravenous drip is used to help this little boy recover from a urinary tract infection.

ulcers

See Mouth problems, page 46.

unconsciousness

See Head injuries, page 38.

urinary tract infections

A urinary tract infection can affect the urethra (causing urethritis), the bladder (causing cystitis) and/or the kidneys (causing pyelonephritis). In newborns, boys are more susceptible than girls to such infections; in older babies, girls are more likely to suffer. It is important that urinary tract infections are treated promptly as they can lead to scarring of the kidneys.

Causes are many but the most frequent is bacteria from the rectum entering the urethra. Girls are more susceptible than boys because their urethra is shorter; this is why it is very important to wipe or clean a girl's anus from front to back, that is, away from the vaginal opening.

In children under two, the symptoms are similar to many other infections, and include fever, diarrhoea, vomiting and lack of energy. If you think your baby may have a urinary tract infection – or if he is unwell and there is no apparent cause – it is important to seek medical advice. If an infection is found, antibiotics will be prescribed.

urticaria

See Hives, page 41.

vaginal infections

In a newborn girl a discharge of mucus from the vagina is normal in the first two weeks, as is occasional spotting of blood. In an older baby or child a vaginal discharge that is smelly or seems to be causing soreness or pain can be caused by bubble baths or poor hygiene.
A discharge can also be caused by worm infestation. It is important that you take your daughter for a medical checkup if you suspect a vaginal infection or notice anything unusual about vaginal discharge.

viruses

There are untold numbers of viruses that can cause infection, so diagnosis can be difficult. Immunity against one virus does not give immunity against another, thus babies and young children, particularly those who spend time with a number of different people, can seem to go from one viral infection to the next. A virus cannot be treated with antibiotics, but a checkup will eliminate other illnesses.

(See Colds, page 23, Influenza, page 42.)

vomiting

It is important not to confuse vomiting in babies under 12 months with possetting, which is the regurgitation of milk. Possetting is common and harmless, and babies grow out of it. Real vomiting is also common – and if it is only one episode is not usually anything to worry about. However, if baby vomits more than once and other symptoms are present, you need to talk to your doctor. If baby is also unusually drowsy, refusing food and has diarrhoea, he is likely to have gastroenteritis (see page 36) and urgent medical attention is vital.

If baby is vomiting after every feed the cause could be pyloric stenosis (see Intestinal obstruction, page 42), which is also a medical emergency.

If he is unusually drowsy and refusing to drink, but does not have diarrhoea, he could have roseola infantum (see page 50) or meningitis (see page 44).

If baby also has a cough, he could have bronchiolitis (see page 18) or whooping cough (see page 57).

If he seems to bring up a large amount of milk after every feed and there are no other symptoms, apart from unhappiness, he could have gastric reflux (see page 36).

whooping cough

Caused by a bacterial infection, whooping cough, or pertussis, is potentially fatal, particularly in babies under six months of age. Immunisation campaigns in the industrialised countries have reduced the number of babies and children who contract the infection, but low rates of infection will only continue as long as children continue to be immunised (see page 8). Whooping cough is so named because of the cough, which consists of a fit of coughing followed by a whooping sound made by air being forced in while the larynx is in spasm and partly closed. Young babies do not always whoop and will suffer from a shortage of oxygen very quickly, with their skin turning a blue-grey colour. The child may also vomit, which can then lead to dehydration. Other possible complications are pneumonia, lung damage, ear problems and convulsions – whooping cough always requires urgent medical attention.

If you suspect whooping cough – and children who are not yet fully immunised are susceptible – seek medical attention urgently. Your child may or may not require hospitalisation, depending on the severity of the case, but medical supervision over the course of the illness is important.

worms

There are many different types of worms which cause parasitic infections but the most common in countries with temperate climates are threadworms (or pinworms) which live in the intestines. If one member of the family is infested, other family members are also likely to be infested. Babies can easily catch threadworms by sucking objects or eating food contaminated with worm eggs. The eggs hatch in the intestines and the adult females emerge from the rectum in the dark and lay eggs round the anus. These worms live only in humans – not in household pets. Symptoms are mainly an itch round the anus and, in girls, an itchy vulva. Sometimes tiny white worms can be seen in the faeces. If you suspect threadworms, you need to take your child to the doctor. The entire family will need to be treated with an antiparasitic medicine, taken in two doses.

In tropical areas, roundworms, which resemble a white earthworm, may be a problem. The main symptom is an appearance of being undernourished. Medication is available from a pharmacist, though a checkup with a doctor is a wise precaution.

Ringworm is caused by a fungal infection, not a worm, and is rarely, if ever, a problem in babies under 12 months.

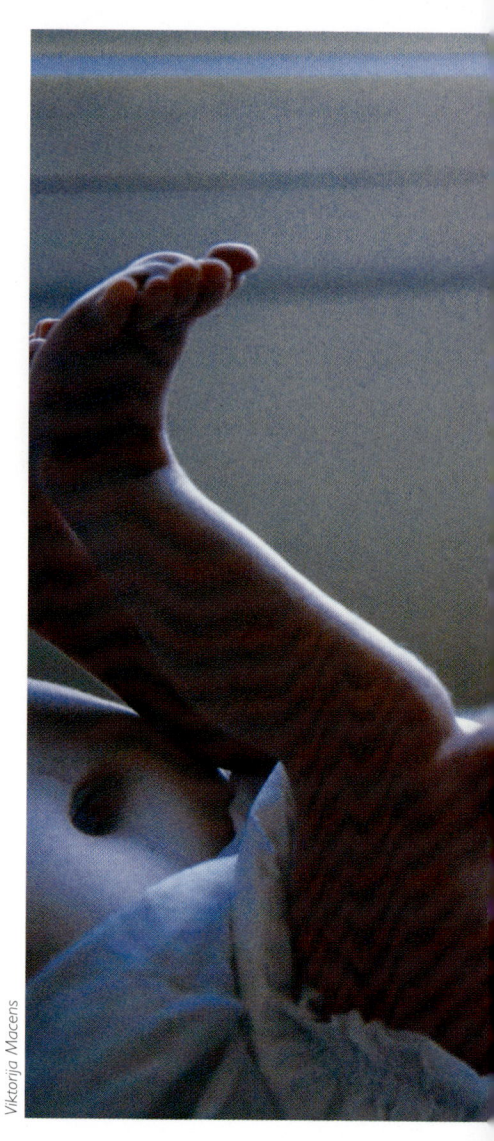

WORMS 59

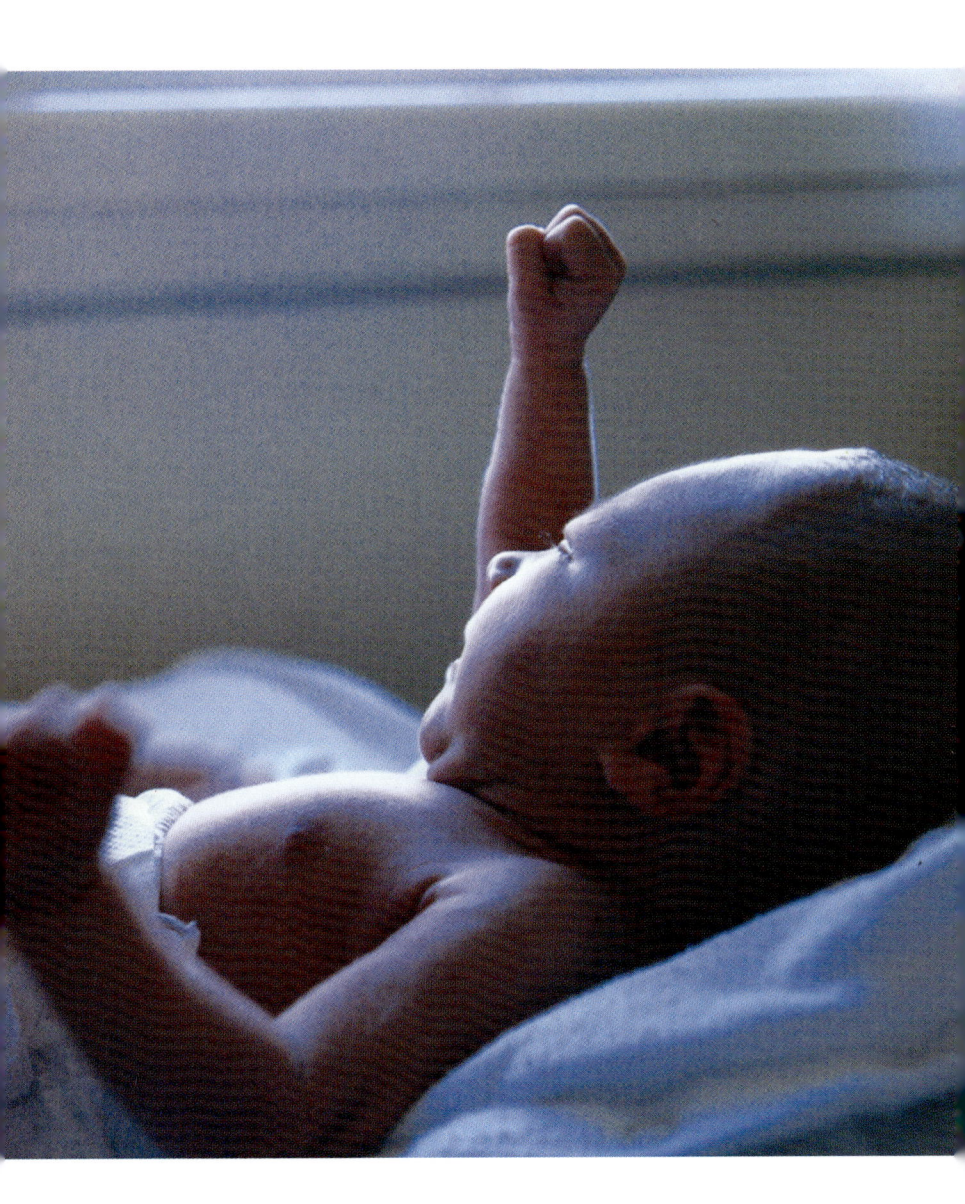

help

important phone numbers

EMERGENCY **000**

POISONS INFORMATION CENTRE **13 11 26**

first aid

Having a current first aid certificate will help you to cope if an emergency strikes and give you some peace of mind as your baby grows and explores.

First aid can save lives and prevent serious injuries. Contact the Australian Red Cross or St John Ambulance for details of courses.

EARLY CHILDHOOD CENTRES

The **Early Childhood Centres** referred to in this book are known by this name in New South Wales – in other states they may go under other names such as Child Health Clinic, or even Maternal and Child Health Clinic. Contact your local council.

BOOKS

Children's Symptoms: The Quick-Reference Guide to Indentification and Treatment including Essential First Aid, by Dr Bernard Valman, Dorling Kindersley, Sydney 1998.

The Parents' When-Not-To-Worry Book, by Carol Fallows, Doubleday, Sydney 2001.

First Aid for Children Fast: Emergency Procedures for all Parents and Carers, with St John Ambulance Australia, Dorling Kindersley, Sydney 1999.

nutrition

BOOKS

Any book by Annabel Karmel, particularly **Feeding Your Baby and Toddler**, Dorling Kindersley, Sydney 1999.

Breast, Bottle, Bowl, by Anne Hillis and Penelope Stone, HarperCollins, Sydney 1999.

Babies and Toddlers Good Food, AWW Cookbooks, Sydney 1999.

Baby Food, by Carol Fallows, Australian Women's Weekly Parenting Guides, Sydney 2001.

WEBSITES

The New Children's Hospital, Westmead, Sydney: **www.nch.edu.au**

advice and information

Your early childhood clinic or infant health centre or maternal and child health centre (the names are different in different places, but your local council should be able to help you find yours) can offer general advice on health concerns.

ADVICE AND INFORMATION ON CHILD SAFETY

Kidsafe (Child Accident Prevention Foundation) has leaflets, books and advice on every aspect of child safety; they can answer many of your questions.

ACT Kidsafe Centre, phone (02) 6290 2244

NSW Child Accident Prevention Foundation of Australia (CAPFA), Kidsafe House, The New Children's Hospital, Westmead, phone (02) 9845 0890

NT Kidsafe, Darwin, phone (08) 8985 1085

Qld CAPFA QLD, Kidsafe House, phone (07) 3854 1829

SA CAPFA SA, Kidsafe Centre, phone (08) 8204 6318

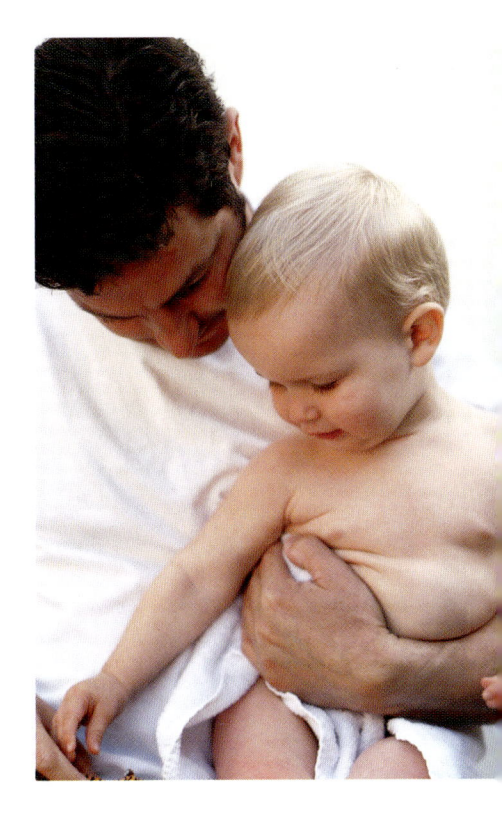

Tas Kidsafe, Hobart, phone (03) 6230 8644

Vic Safety Centre, Royal Children's Hospital, phone (03) 9345 5085
Kidsafe, Victoria, phone (03) 9836 4070

WA Kidsafe WA, Princess Margaret Hospital for Children, phone (08) 9340 8509

index

abdominal pain	10	dog bite	14	intestinal obstruction	42	scabies	51
AIDS	41	drowning	28	intussusception	42	scalds	20
allergic rhinitis	10	ears	31, 52	knock-knees	44	scarlet fever	51
allergies	10	eczema	31	lead poisoning	49	school sores	41
anaemia	10	encephalitis	32	leg problems	44	scorpion bite	14
anaphylactic shock	14, 51	expired air resuscitation	21	lockjaw	54	shock	14, 51
ant bite	14	eyes	32	lumps and swellings	44	sneezing	52
antibiotics	12	febrile convulsion	24, 33	marine stings	16	spider bite	16
aspirin	12	feet	34	measles	44	splinters	52
asthma	13, 18	fever	33, 52	meningitis	44	squint	32
bee sting	14	finger injury	34	bacterial	44	SSPE	12
bites and stings	14-17	fits	24	meningococcal	44	strabismus	33
animal bites	14	flea bite	16	viral	44	strangulated hernia	43
insect bites	14	fracture	34	middle ear infection	31	subacute sclerosing panencephalitis	12
blocked tear duct	32	gastric reflux	36	milia	50	suffocation	52
blood in stool	42	gastroenteritis	36	mosquito bite	16	sunburn	52
bow-legs	44	gastro-oesophageal reflux	36	mouth problems	46	swollen glands	44
breathing problems	18	genital problems	37	thrush	46	teething	52
bronchiolitis	18	German measles	50	ulcers	46	temperature	17
bronchitis	18	giardiasis	37	mumps	8, 47	tetanus	54
burns	20	giving medicine	6	nose problems	47	threadworms	58
cat bite	14	head injury	38	otitis media	31	thrush	54
centipede bite	14	heart murmur	38	pertussis	57	tick bite	17
chickenpox	21	heat exhaustion	39	pesticides	49	tooth decay	46
choking	18, 21	heat rash	39	pigeon toes	34	triple antigen	8
club foot	34	heat stroke	39	pinworms	58	urinary tract infections	55
coeliac disease	22	hepatitis	8, 40	pneumonia	47	urticaria	41
colds	23	hernia	40	poisoning	48	vaccination	8
colic	10, 23, 42	inguinal	41	poliomyelitis	48	vaginal infections	56
concussion	38	strangulated	43	pollution effects	49	varicella	21
conjunctivitis	23	umbilical	40	possetting	36, 56	viruses	56
constipation	24	Hib vaccine	8	prickly heat	39, 50	vomiting	10, 32, 37, 38, 45, 52, 56
convulsions	24, 33	HIV	41	pyloric stenosis	43	whooping cough	57
cradle cap	24	hives	41	rash	44, 45, 50	worms	58
croup	18	immunisation	8	Reye's syndrome	12		
dehydration	26, 39	impetigo	41	roseola infantum	50		
diarrhoea	26, 37, 52	influenza	42	roundworms	58		
dislocation	28			rubella	50		
diphtheria	28			Sabin vaccine	8, 48		

Viktorija Macens

Editorial director Susan Tomnay
Senior editor Georgina Bitcon
Editor Anne Savage
Design concept Michele Withers
Designer Mary Keep
Photographer Scott Cameron
Stylist Mary-Anne Danaher
Illustrator Jo McComiskey
Sales manager Jennifer McDonald
Group publisher Jill Baker
Publisher Sue Wannan
Chief executive officer John Alexander

Produced by ACP Books, Sydney.

Colour separations by
ACP Colour Graphics Pty Ltd, Sydney.

Printing by Dai Nippon Printing, Hong Kong

Published by ACP Publishing Pty Limited,
54 Park St, Sydney; GPO Box 4088, Sydney,
NSW 1028. Ph: (02) 9282 8618
Fax: (02) 9267 9438.

To order books, phone 136 116.
acpbooks@acp.com.au
www.acpbooks.com.au

Australia Distributed by Network services,
GPO Box 4088, Sydney, NSW 1028.
Ph: (02) 9282 8777 Fax: (02) 9264 3278.

United Kingdom Distributed by Australian
Consolidated Press (UK), Moulton Park Business
Centre, Red House Road, Moulton Park,
Northampton, NN3 6AQ. Ph: (01604) 497 531
Fax: (01604) 497 533 acpukltd@aol.com

Canada Distributed by Whitecap Books Ltd,
351 Lynn Ave, North Vancouver, BC, V7J 2C4,
Ph: (604) 980 9852.

New Zealand Distributed by Netlink
Distribution Company, Level 4, 23 Hargreaves St,
College Hill, Auckland 1, Ph: (9) 302 7616.

South Africa Distributed by PSD Promotions
(Pty) Ltd, PO Box 1175, Isando 1600, SA,
Ph: (011) 392 6065.

Fallows, Carol.

Baby health.

Includes index.
ISBN 1 86396 225 5.

1. Infants – Health and hygiene. 2. Infants – Care.
I. Title. (Series: Australian Women's Weekly
parenting guides; 4).
649.122

© ACP Publishing Pty Limited 2001
ACN 053 273 546
ABN 18 053 273 546

First published 2001. Reprinted 2002.

This publication is copyright. No part of it may be
reproduced or transmitted in any form without
the written permission of the publishers.

Cover photograph Viktorija Macens
Back cover photograph Scott Cameron

The publishers would like to thank the following for help in preparing this book:

Sydney Children's Hospital, Randwick, NSW, Australia
http://www.sch.edu.au/

NSW Cancer Council, Sydney, Australia

Products used in photographs were supplied by:

Britax Child-Care Products Pty Ltd, Vic, Australia,
phone (03) 9288 7288.

Babyco Direct, Vic, Australia,
phone (03) 9764333

Mattel Pty Ltd, Vic, Australia,
phone (03) 94255222

Baby Bjorn, Vic, Australia,
phone (03) 96450222

Ikea Australia, phone (02) 94182744